Presenting:

POP ART 123's

A COLORFUL COUNTING BOOK

WORDS & ART BY: BRIANNA DAVIS

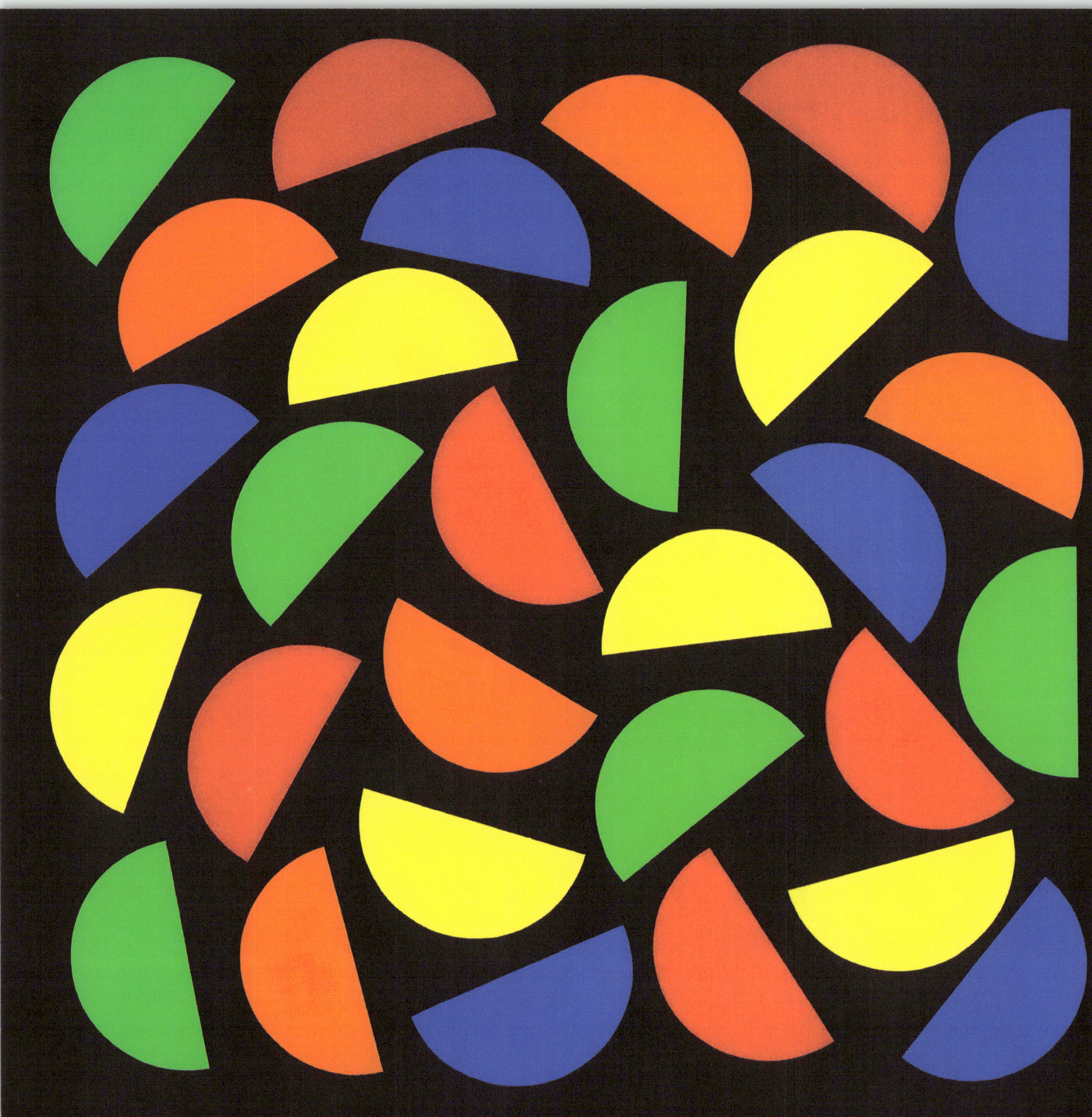

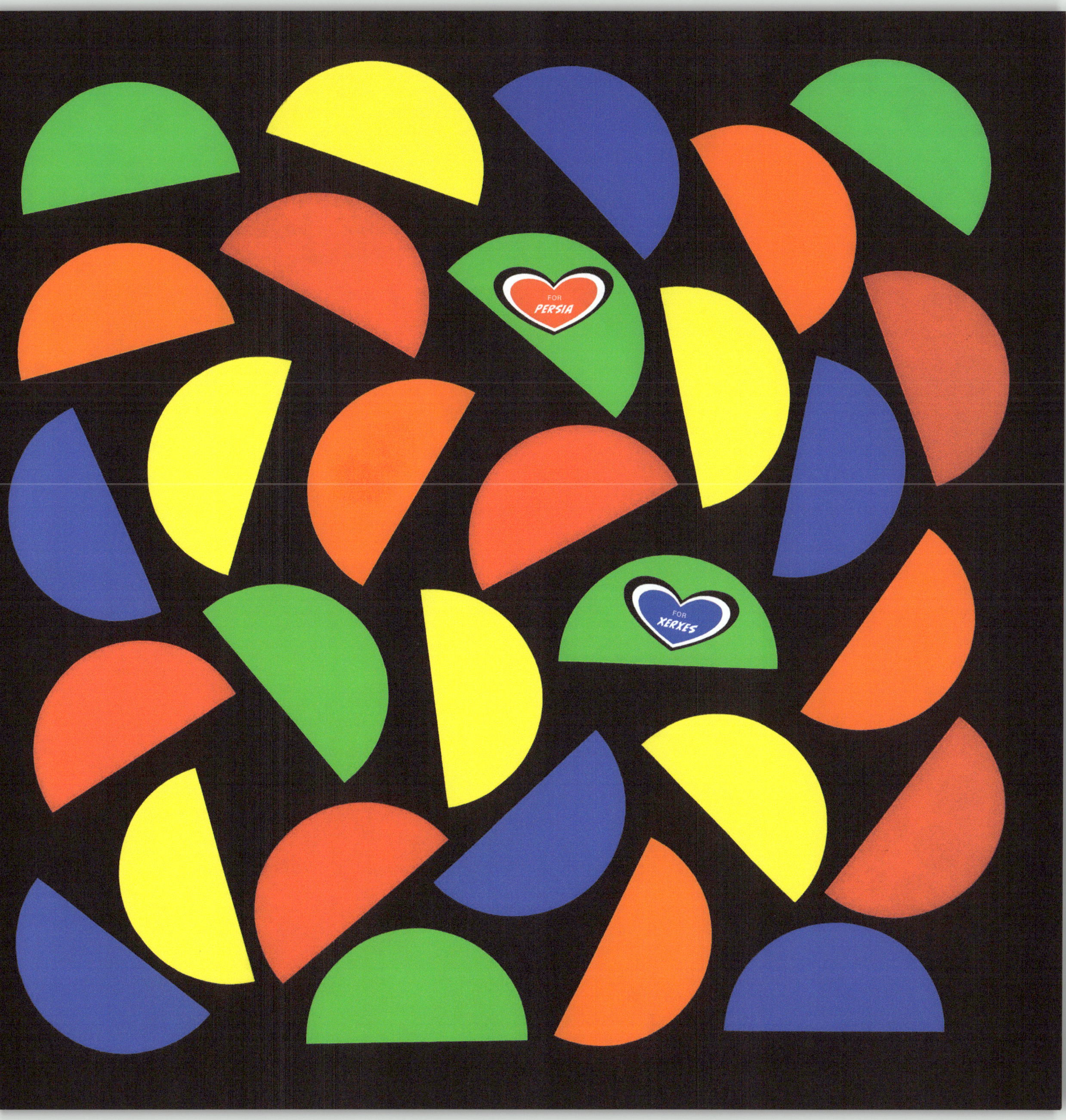
FOR
PERSIA
FOR
XERXES

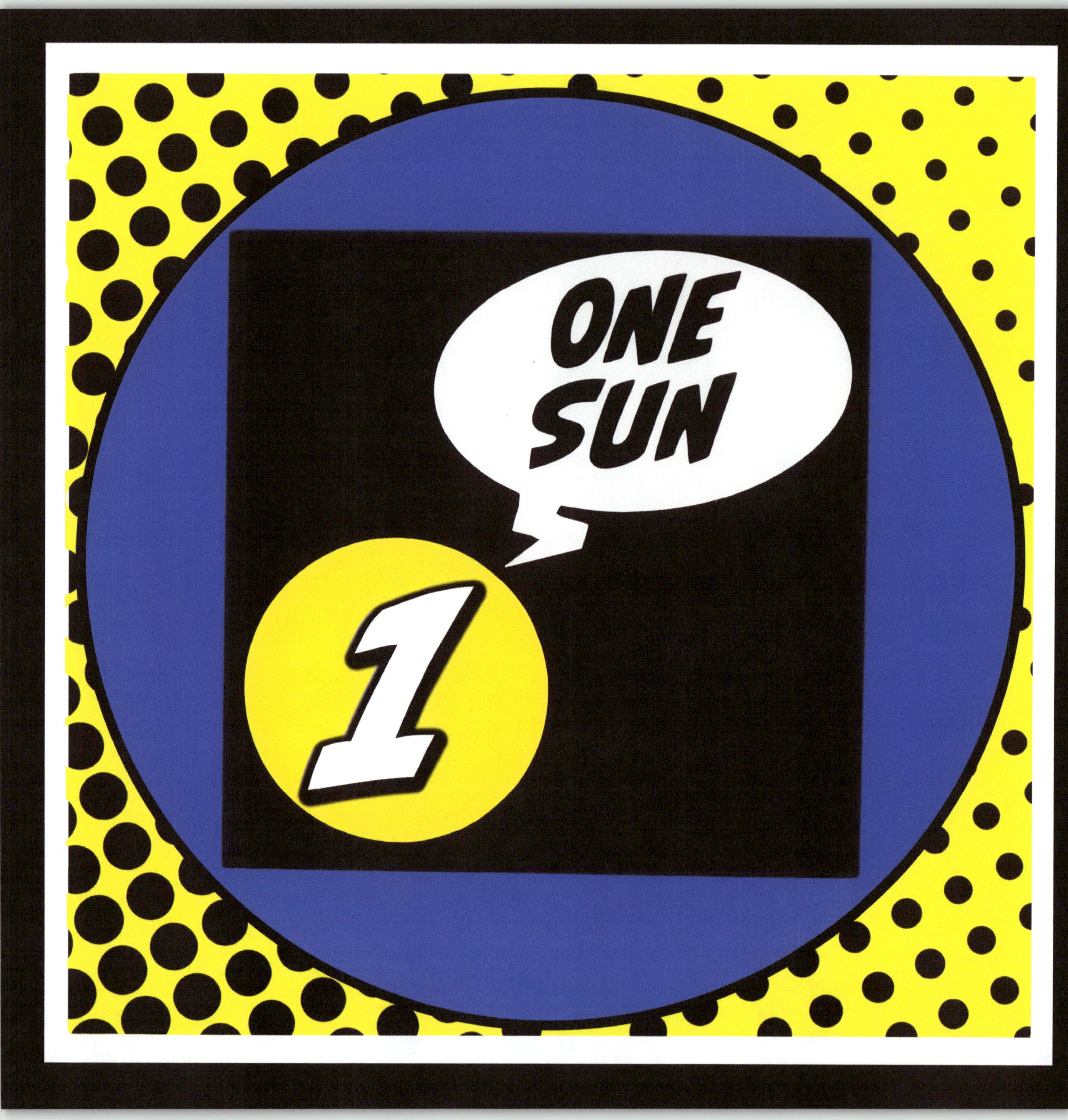
ONE SUN
1

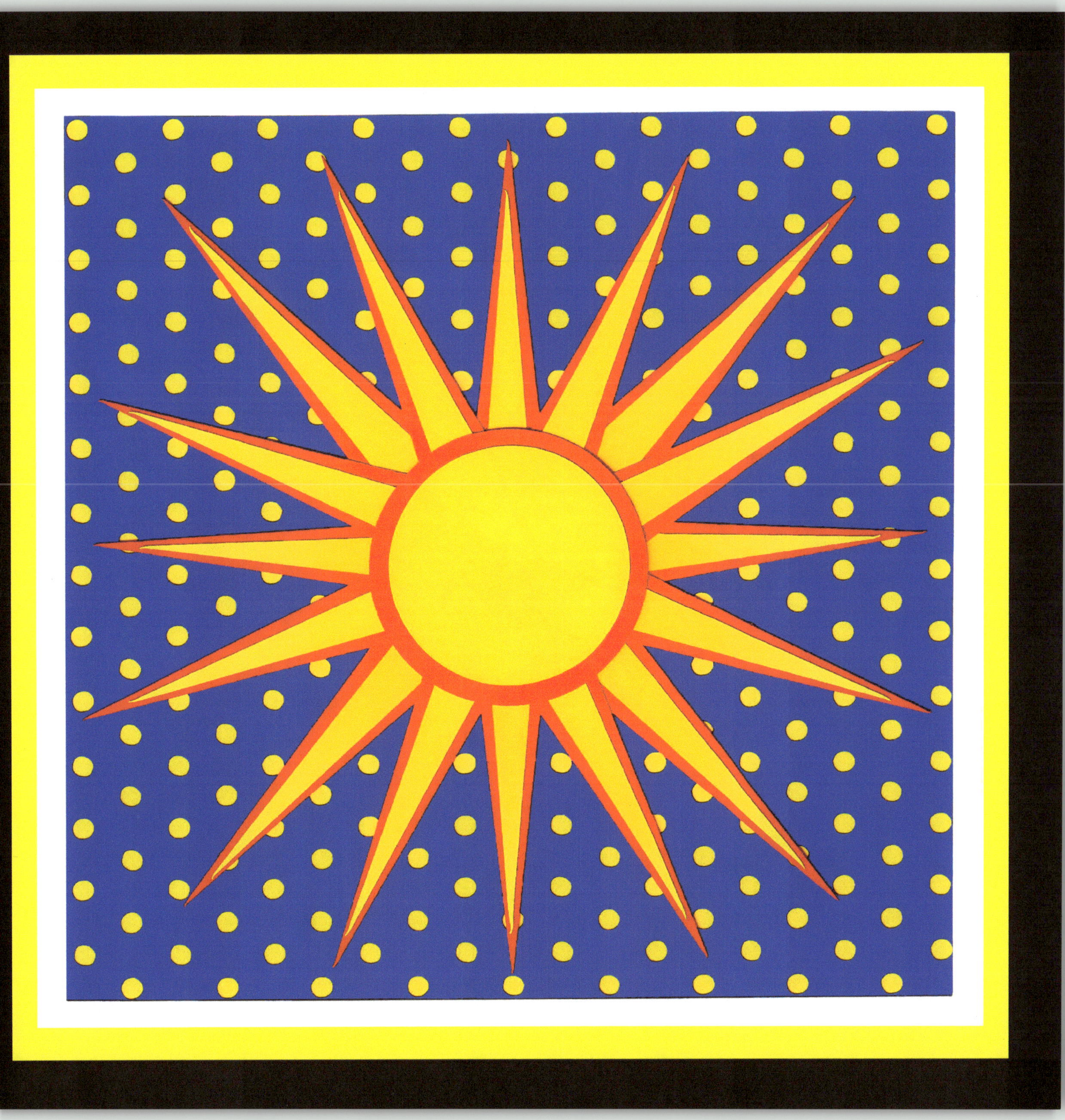

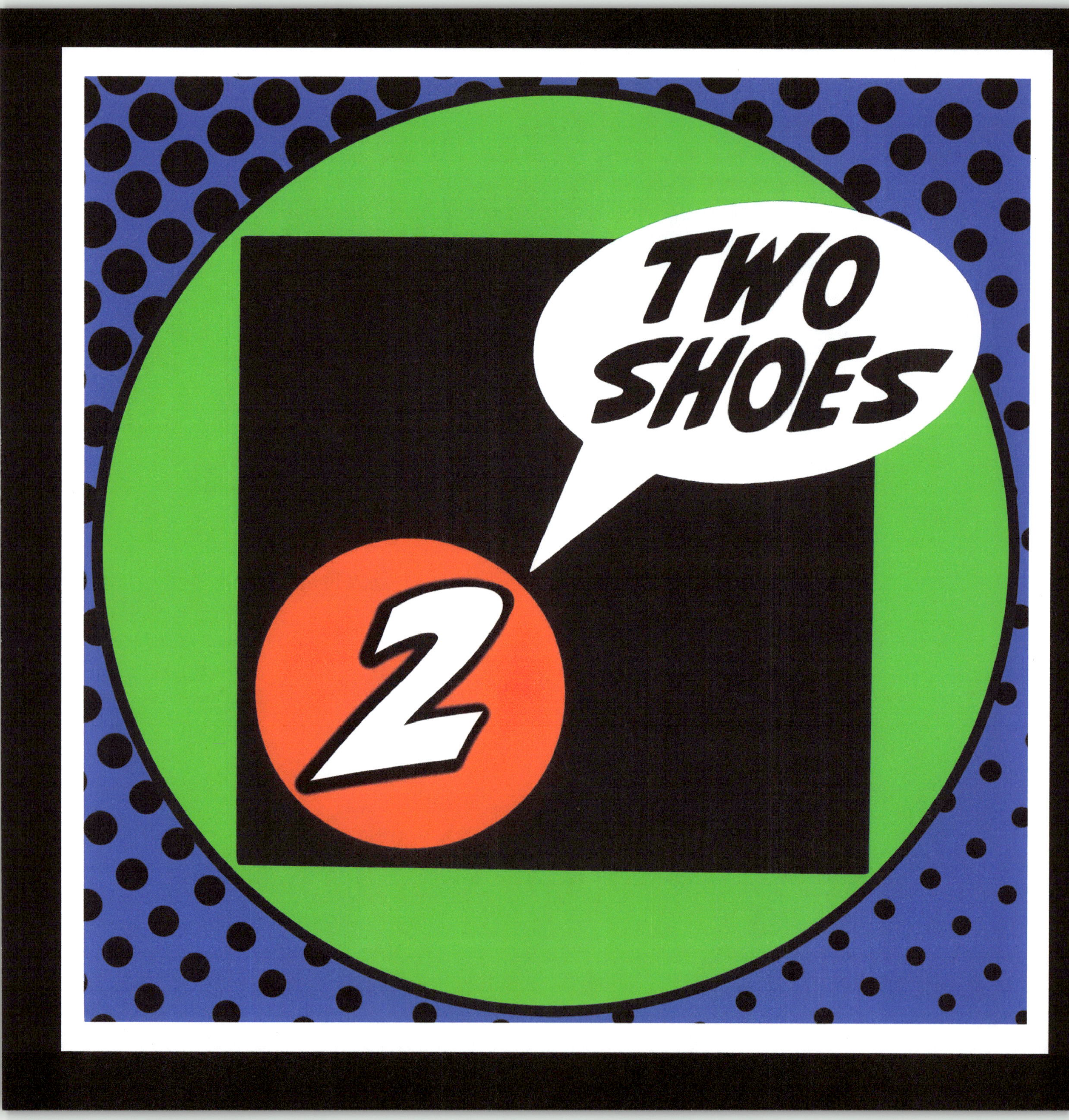
TWO
SHOES
2

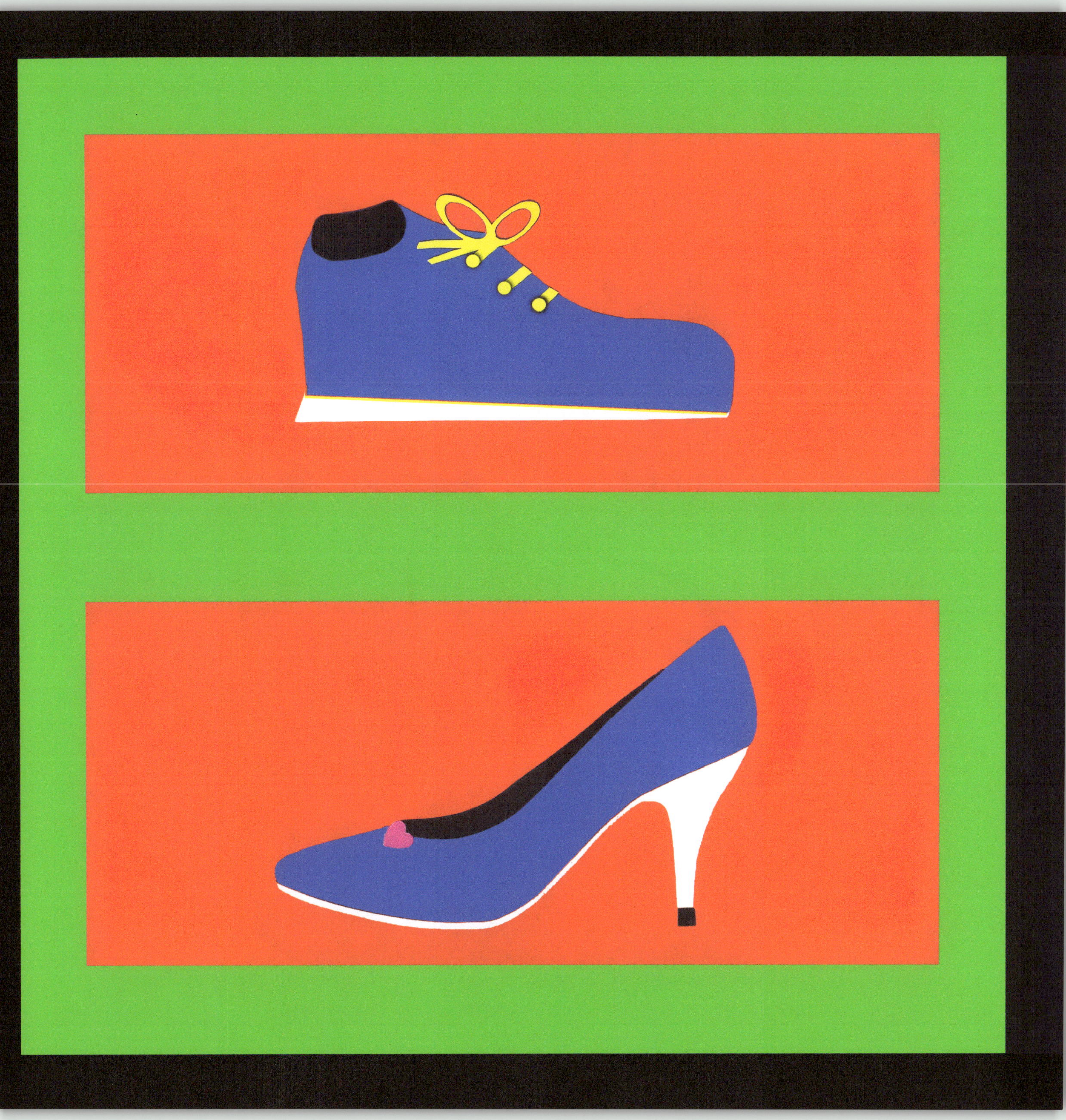

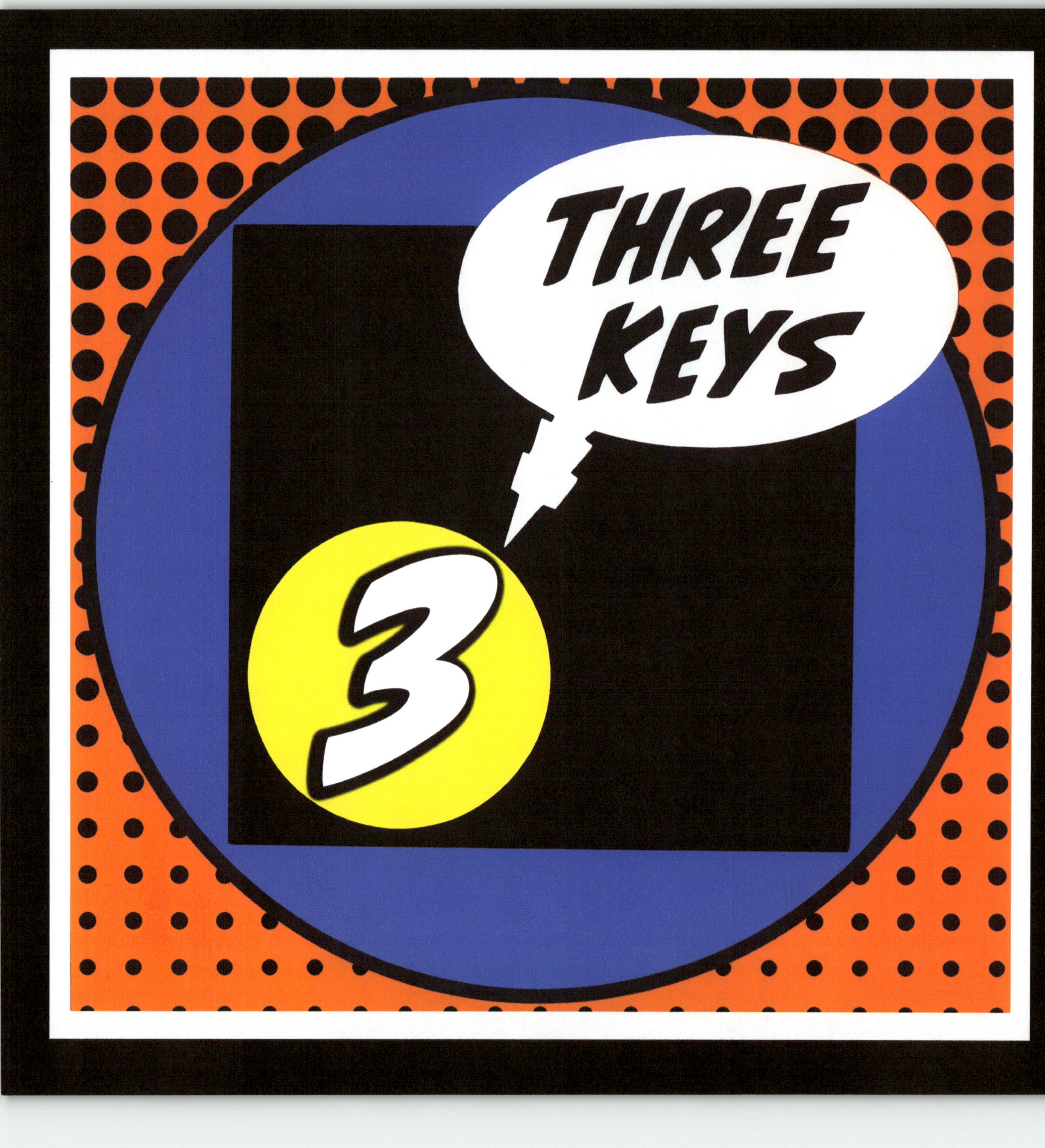
THREE
KEYS
3

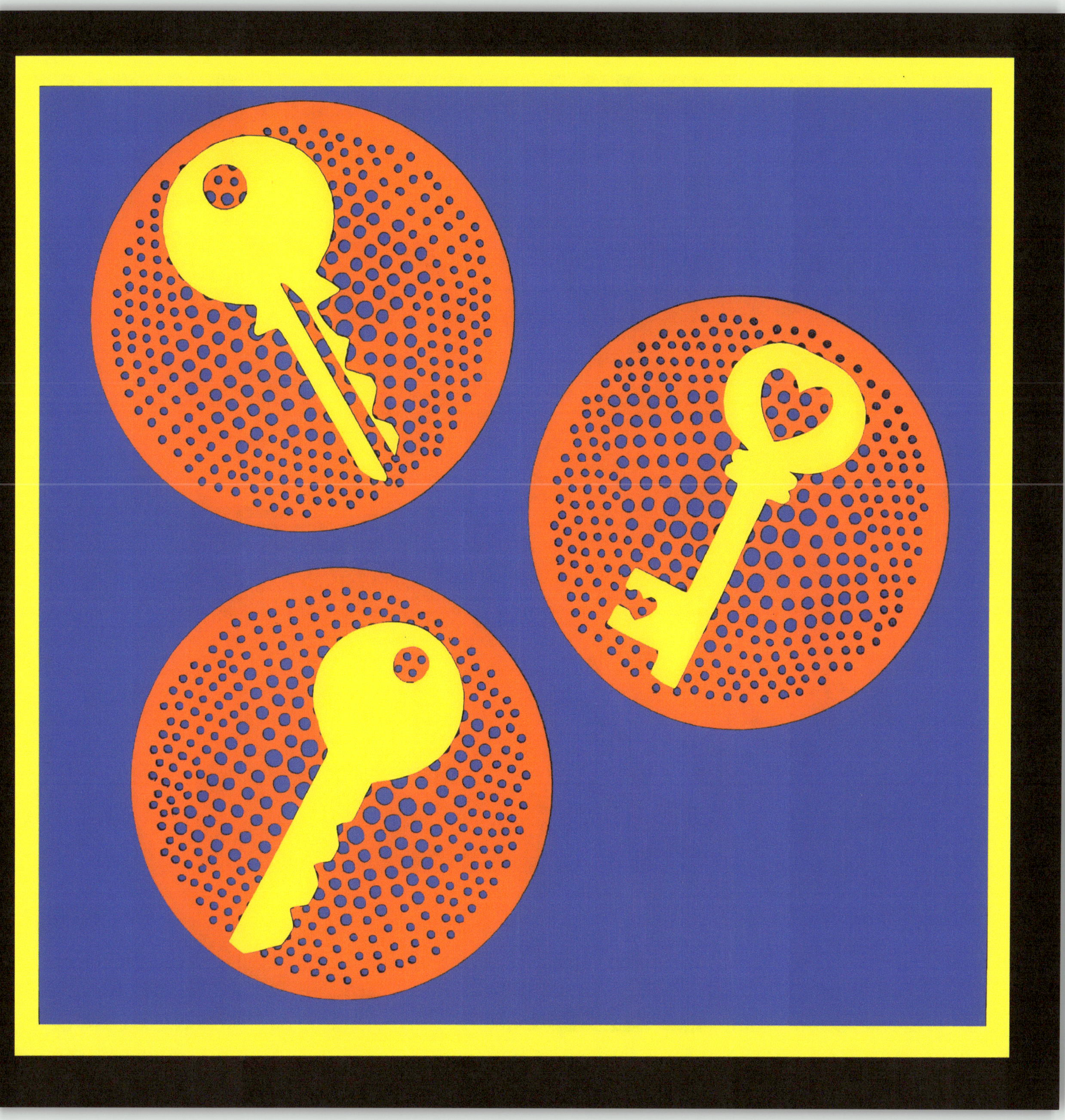

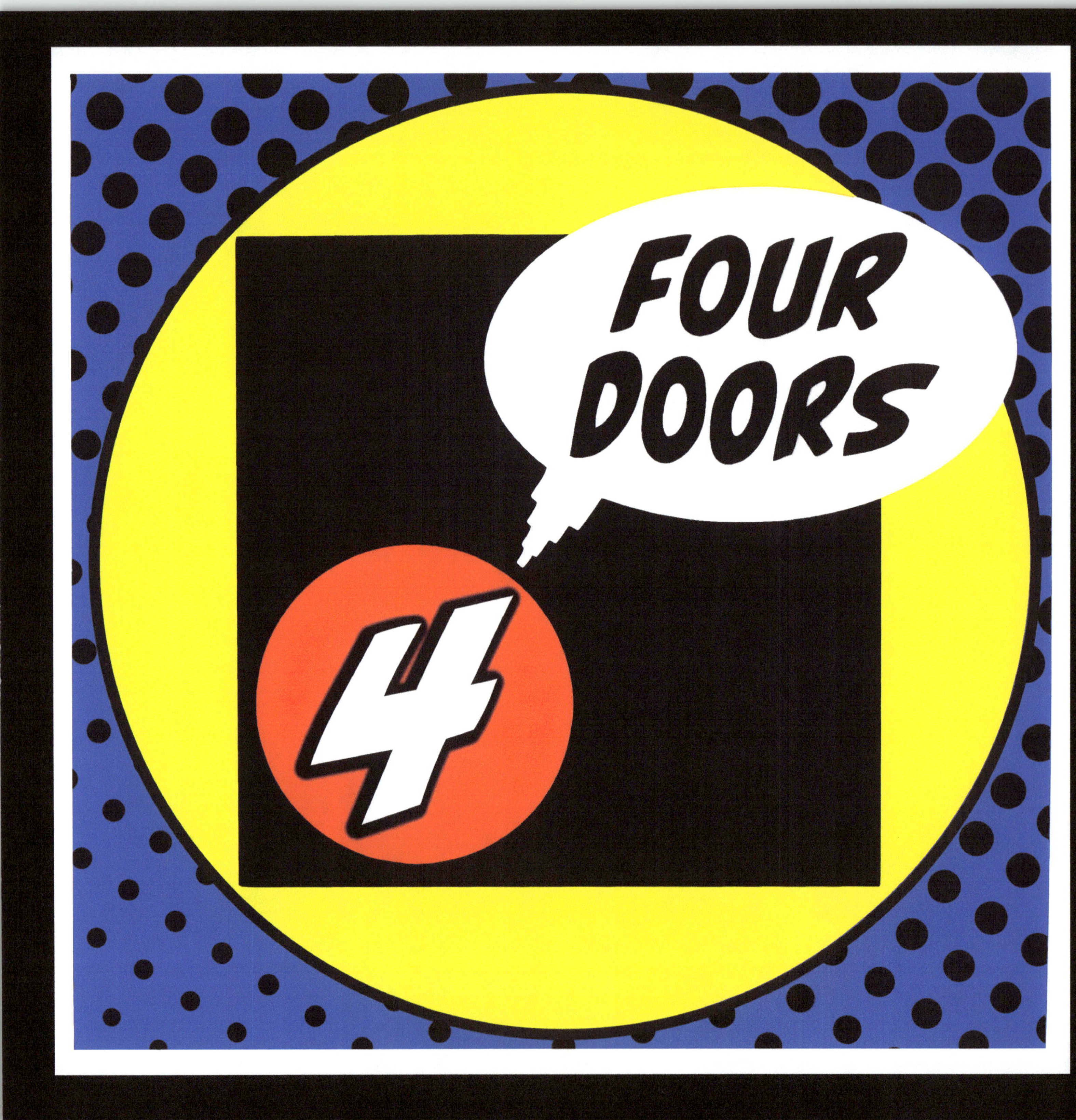
FOUR DOORS
4

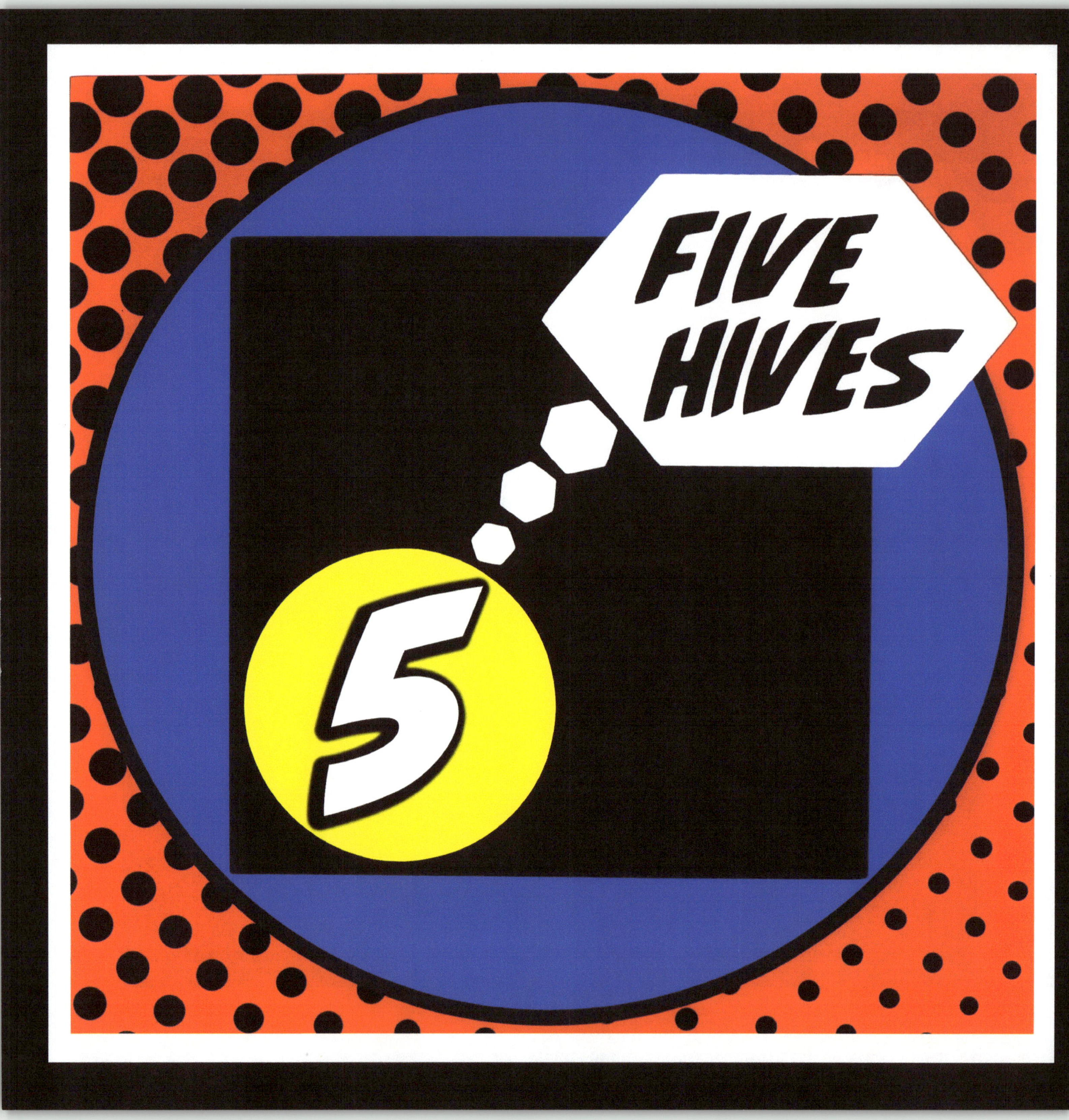
FIVE HIVES
5

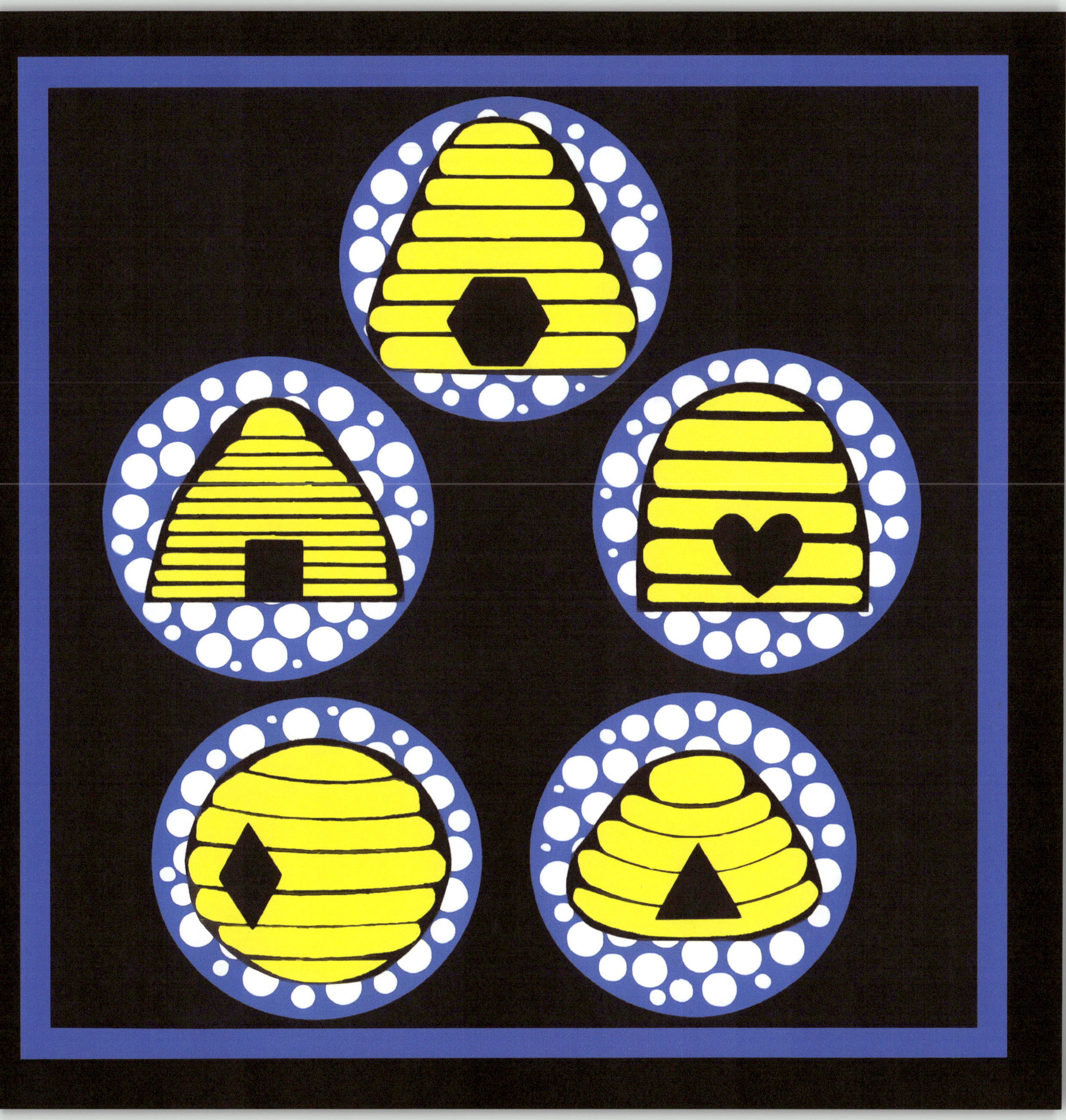

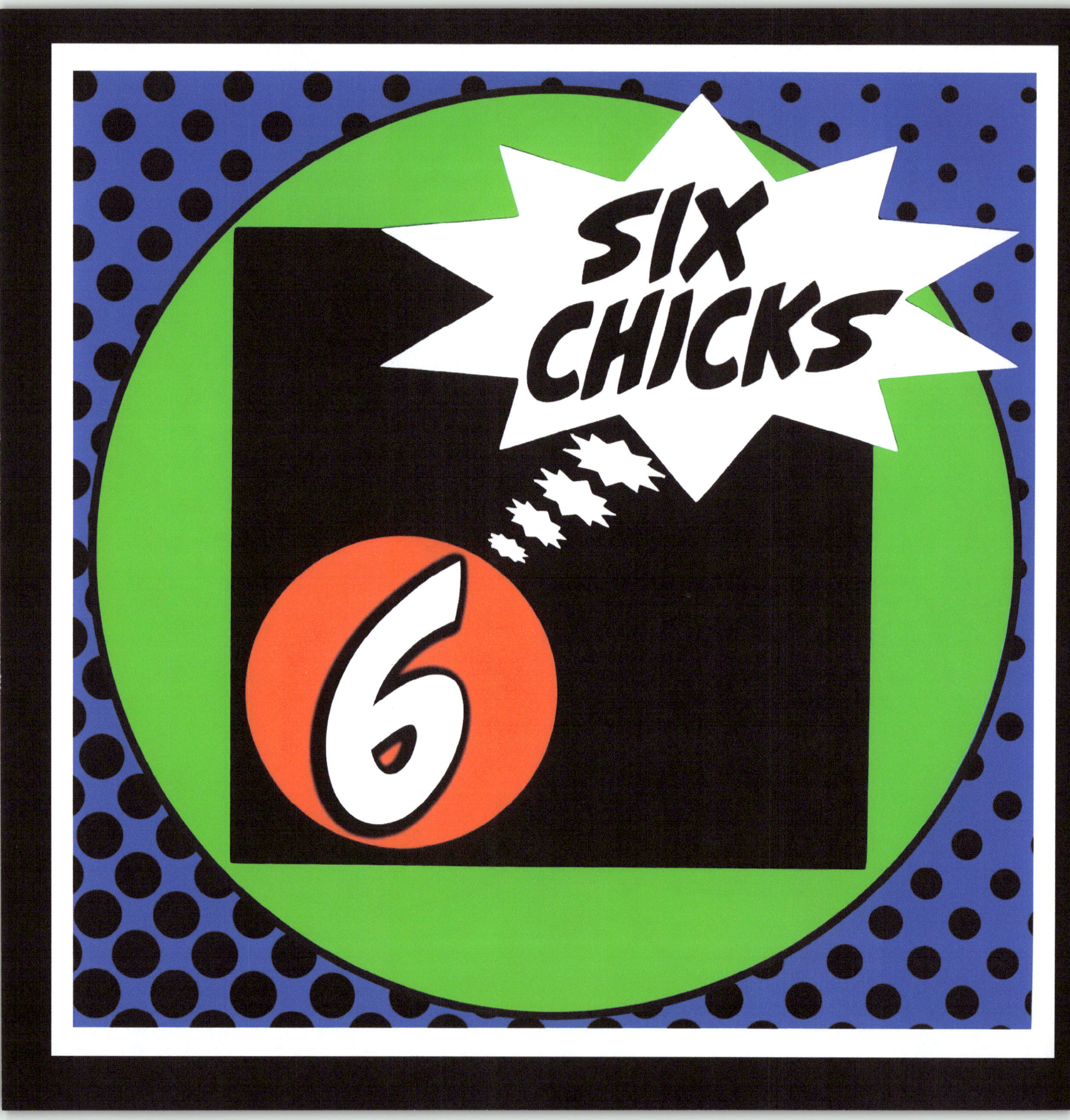
SIX CHICKS
6

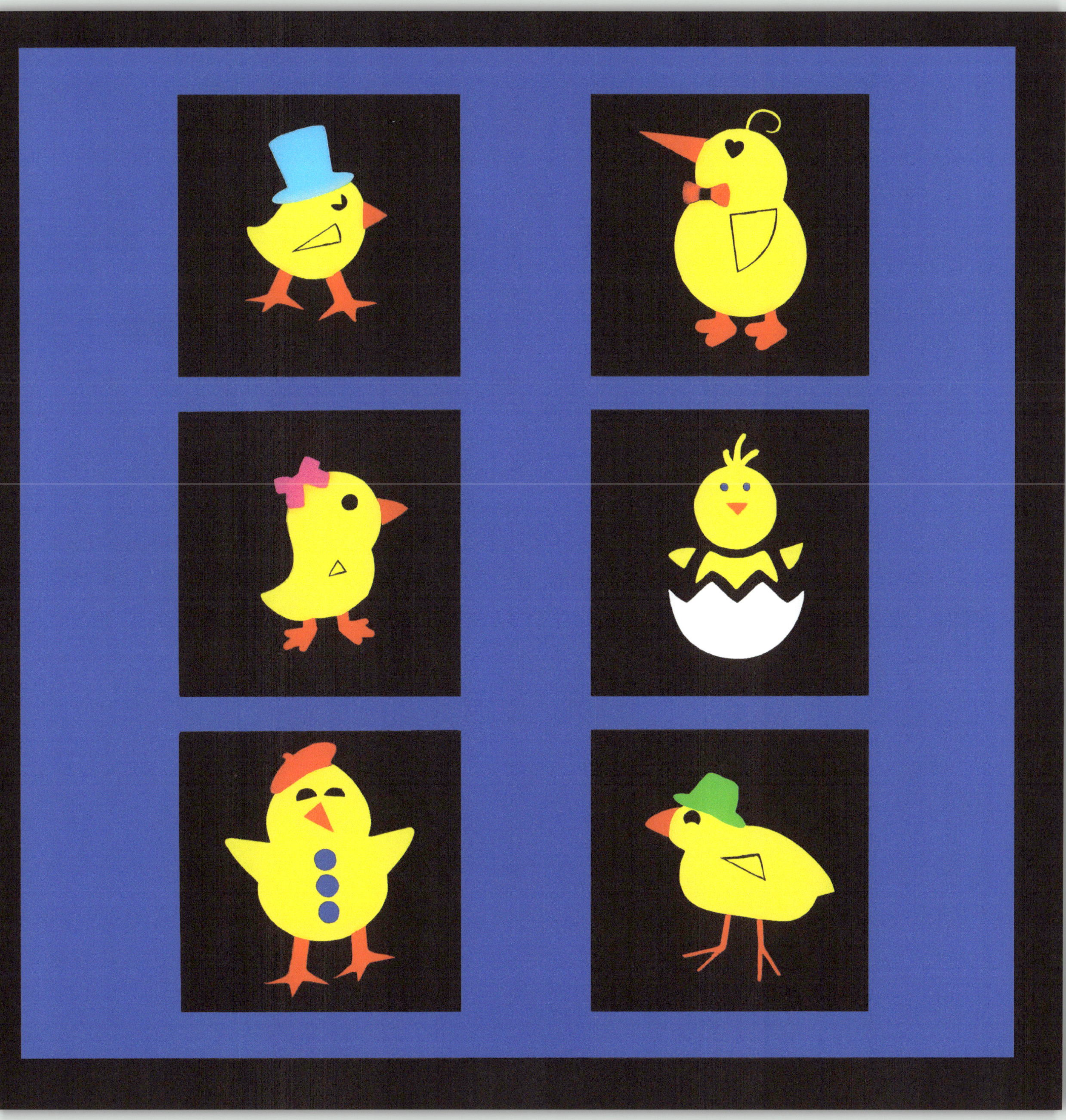

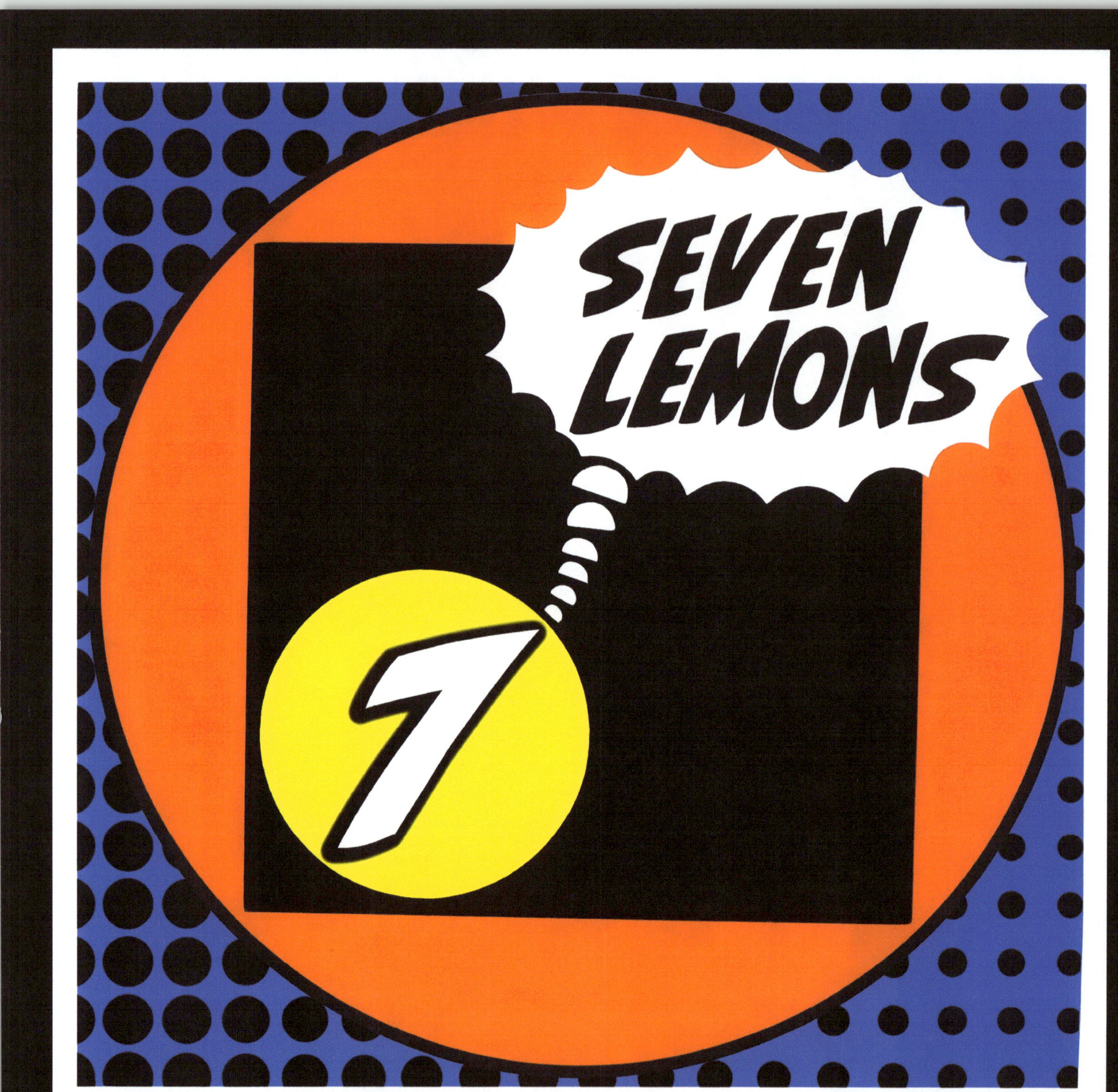
SEVEN
LEMONS
7

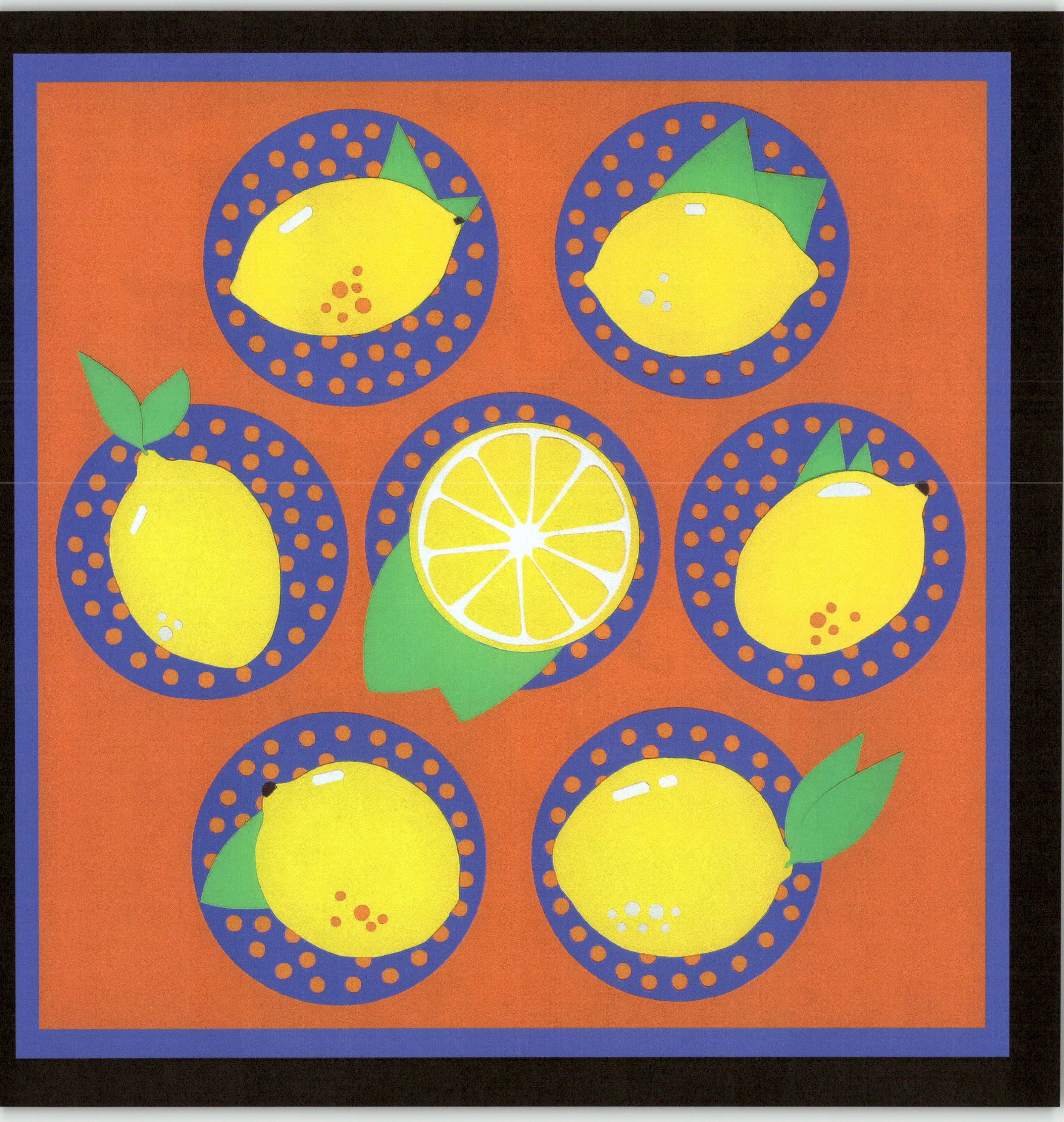

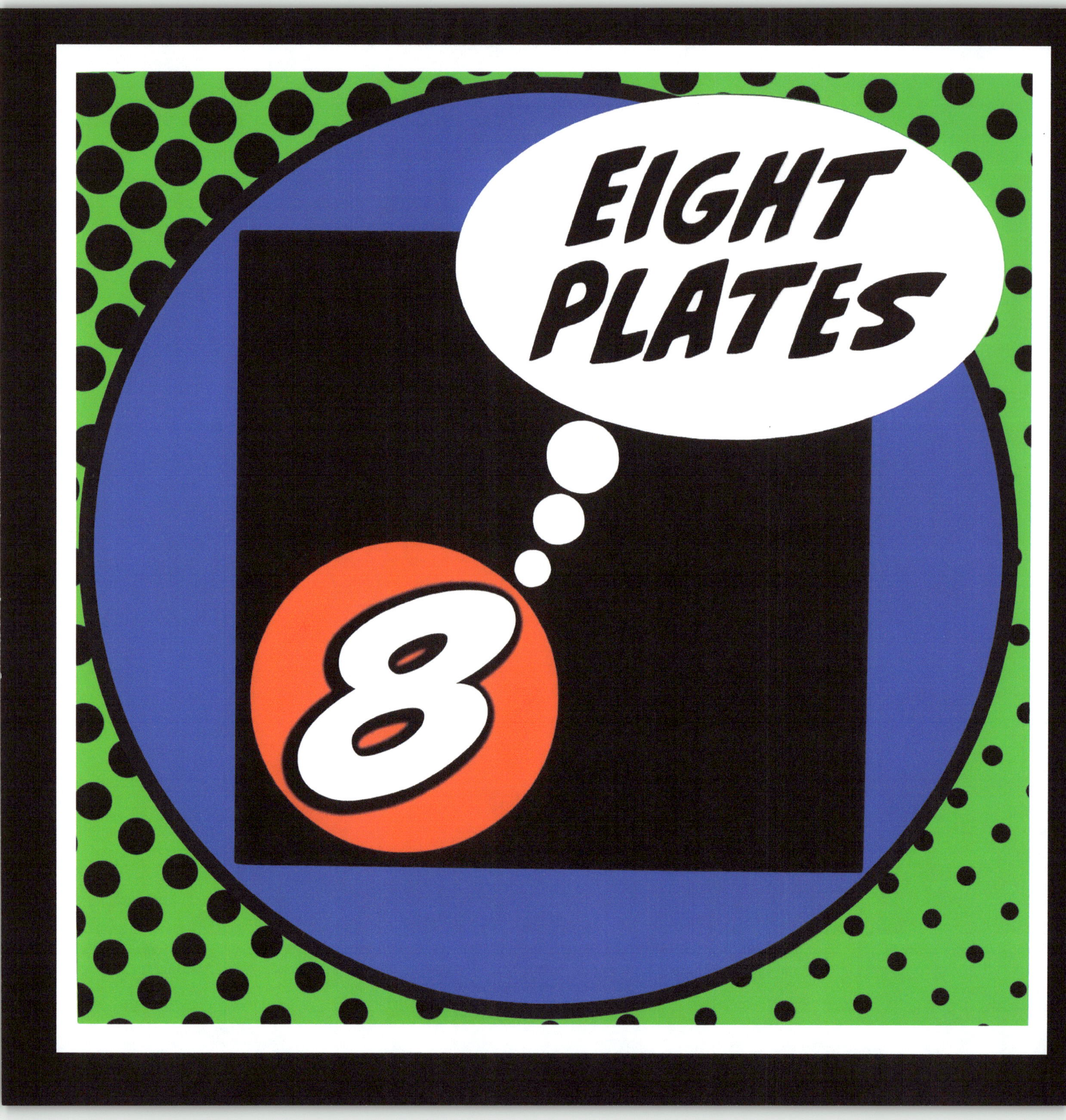
EIGHT PLATES
8

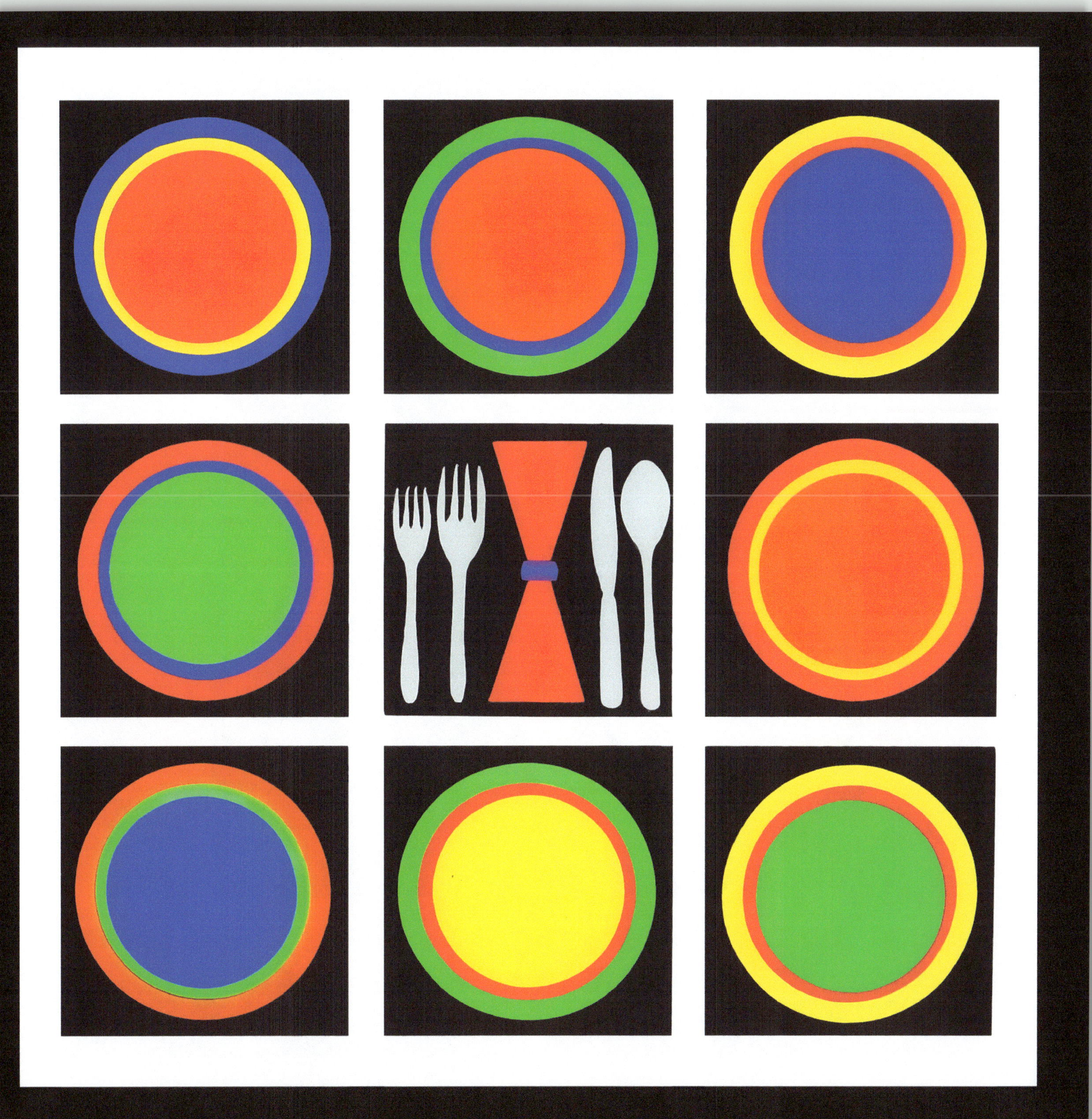

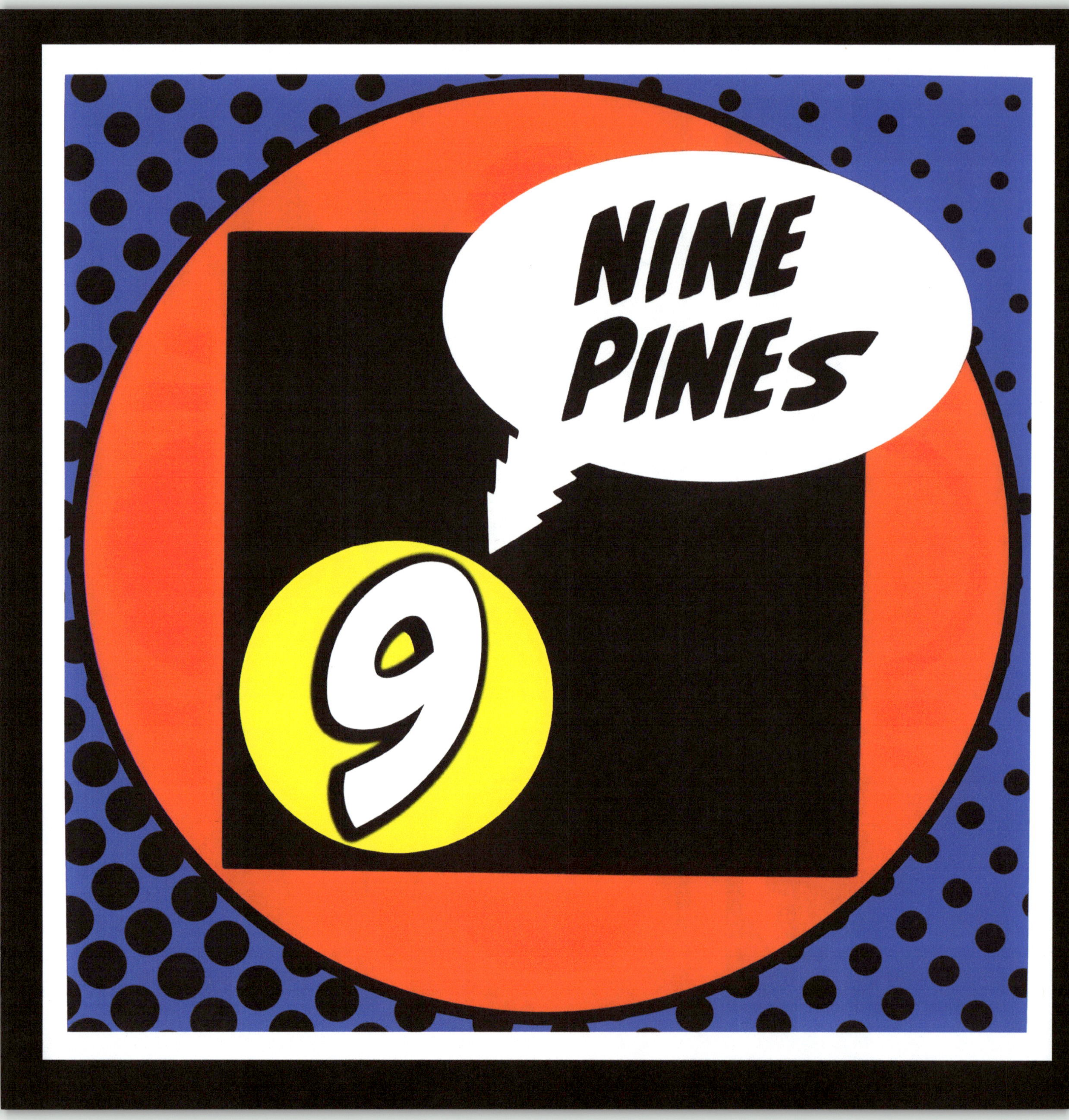
NINE
PINES
9

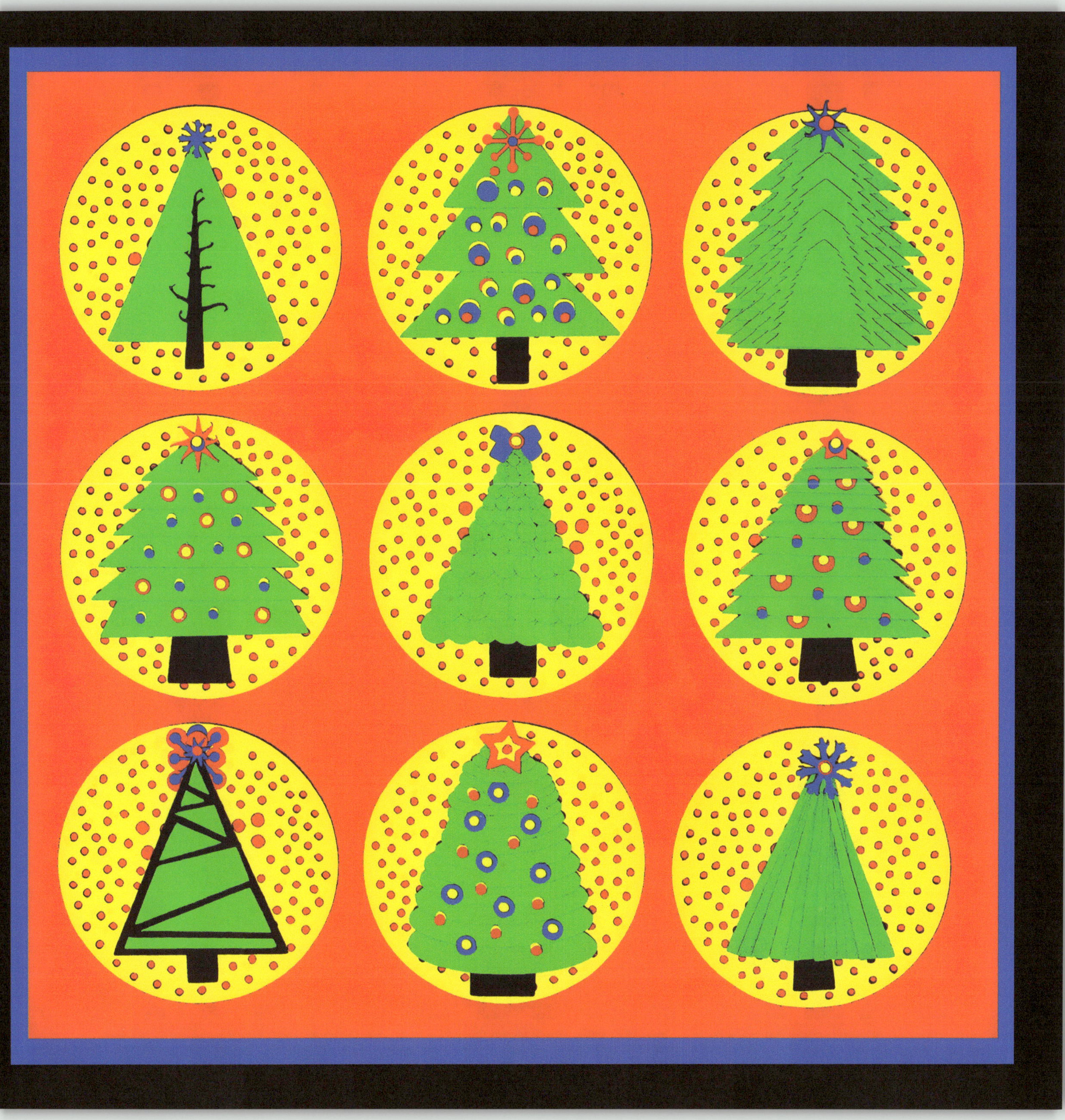

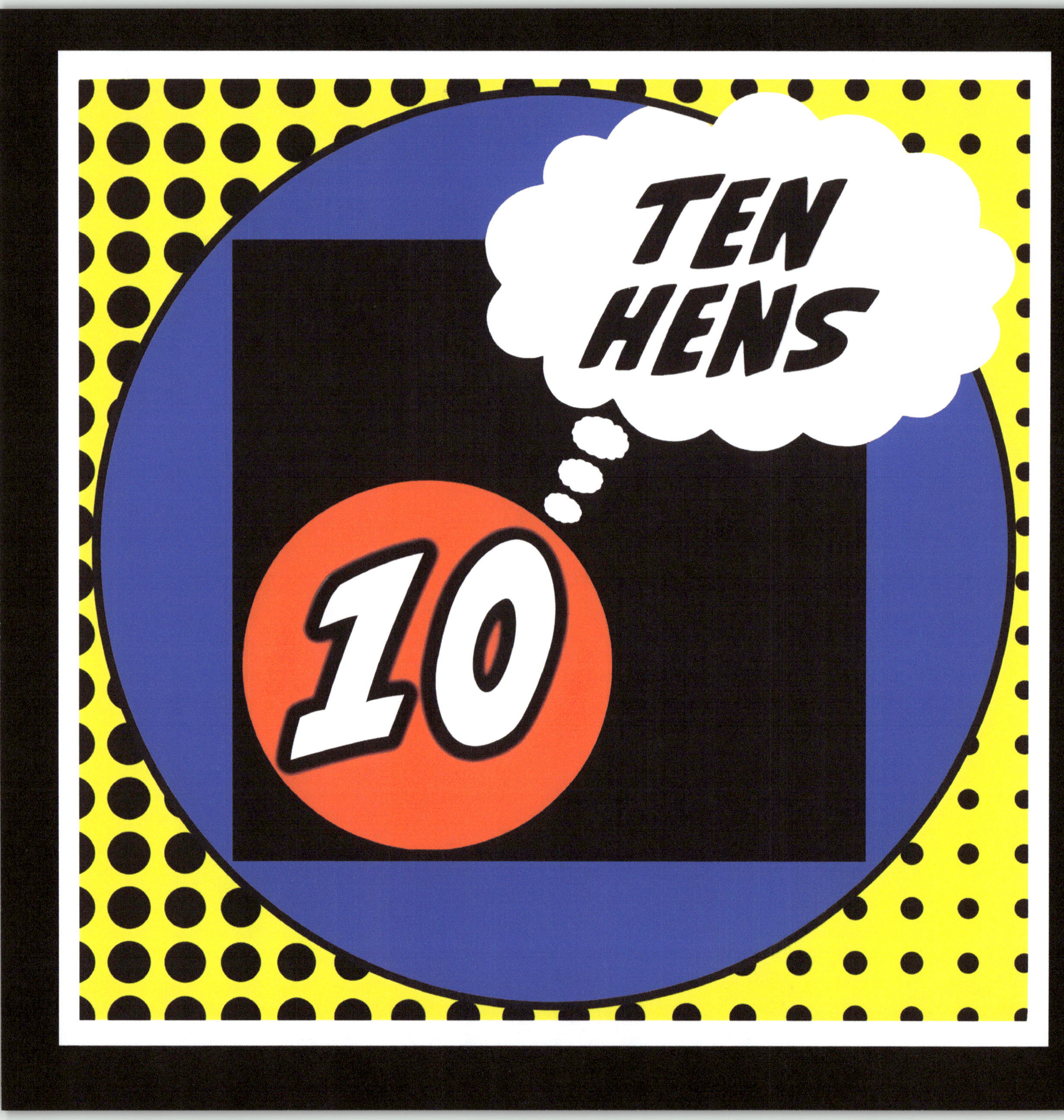
TEN
HENS
10

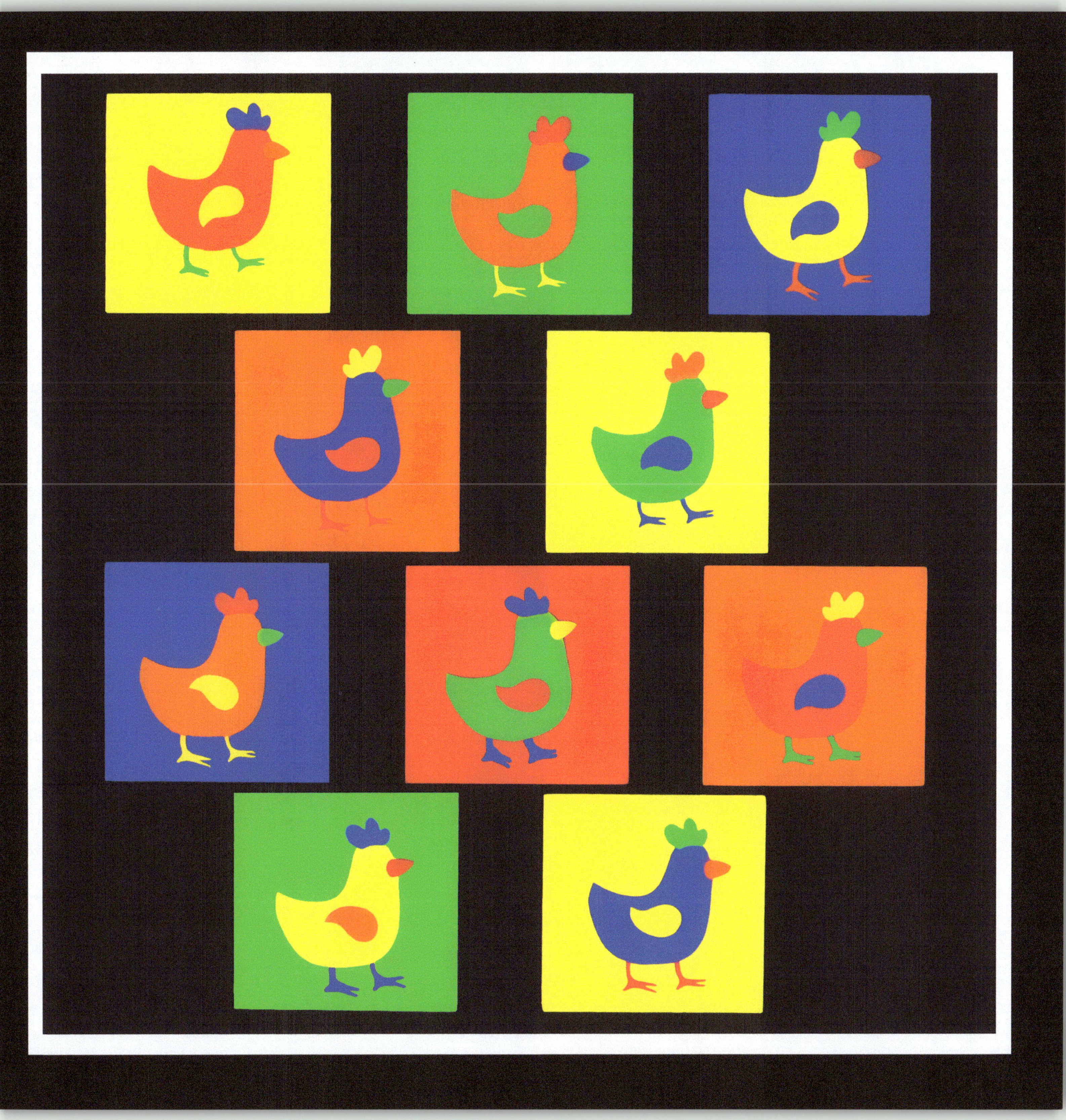

LET'S COUNT AND RHYME ONE MORE TIME!

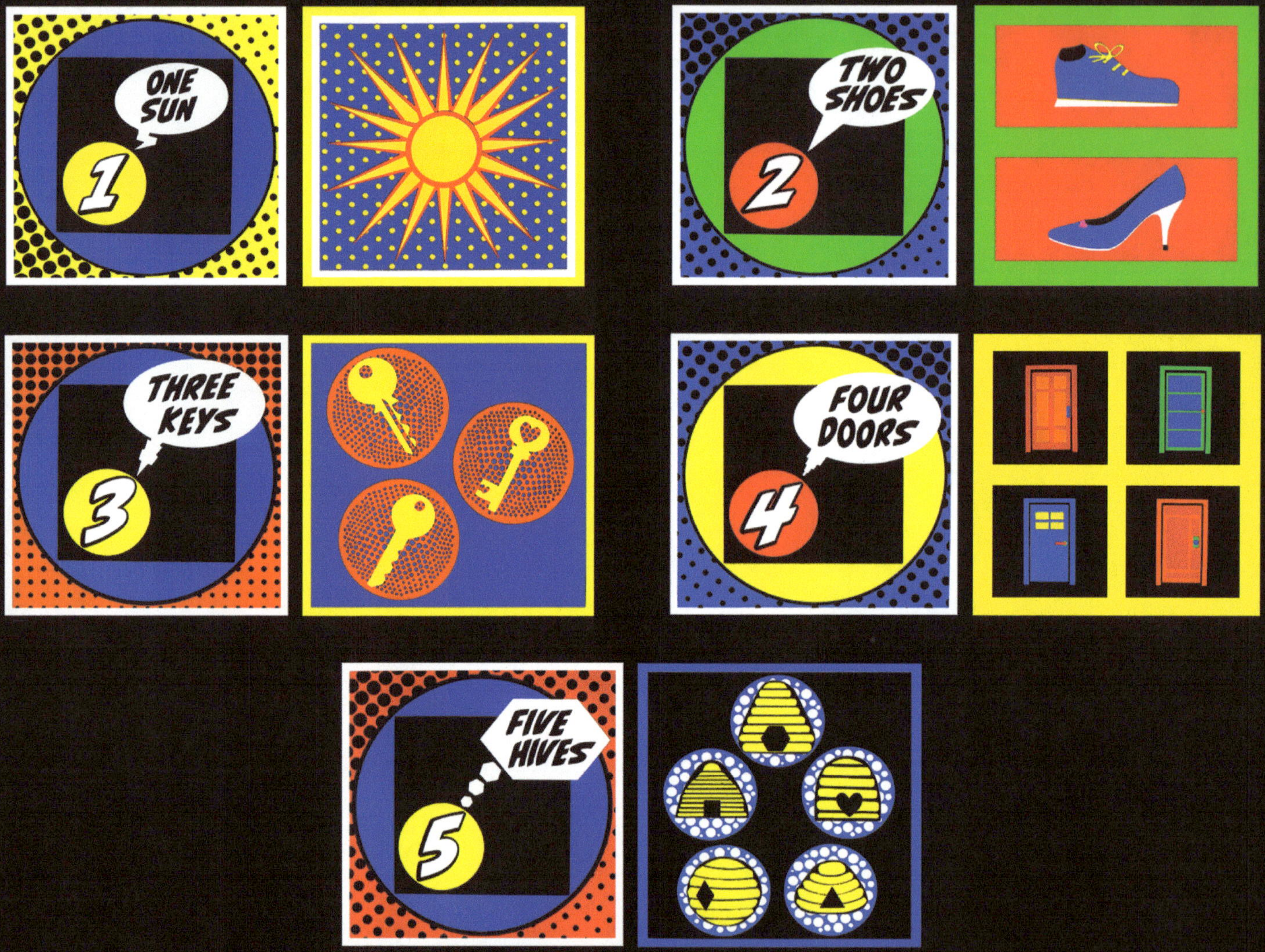
ONE SUN
1
TWO SHOES
2
THREE KEYS
3
FOUR DOORS
4
FIVE HIVES
5

1, 2, 3, 4, 5: WE'RE GOING INTO OVERDRIVE!

NOW FOR 6, 7, 8, 9, AND 10...

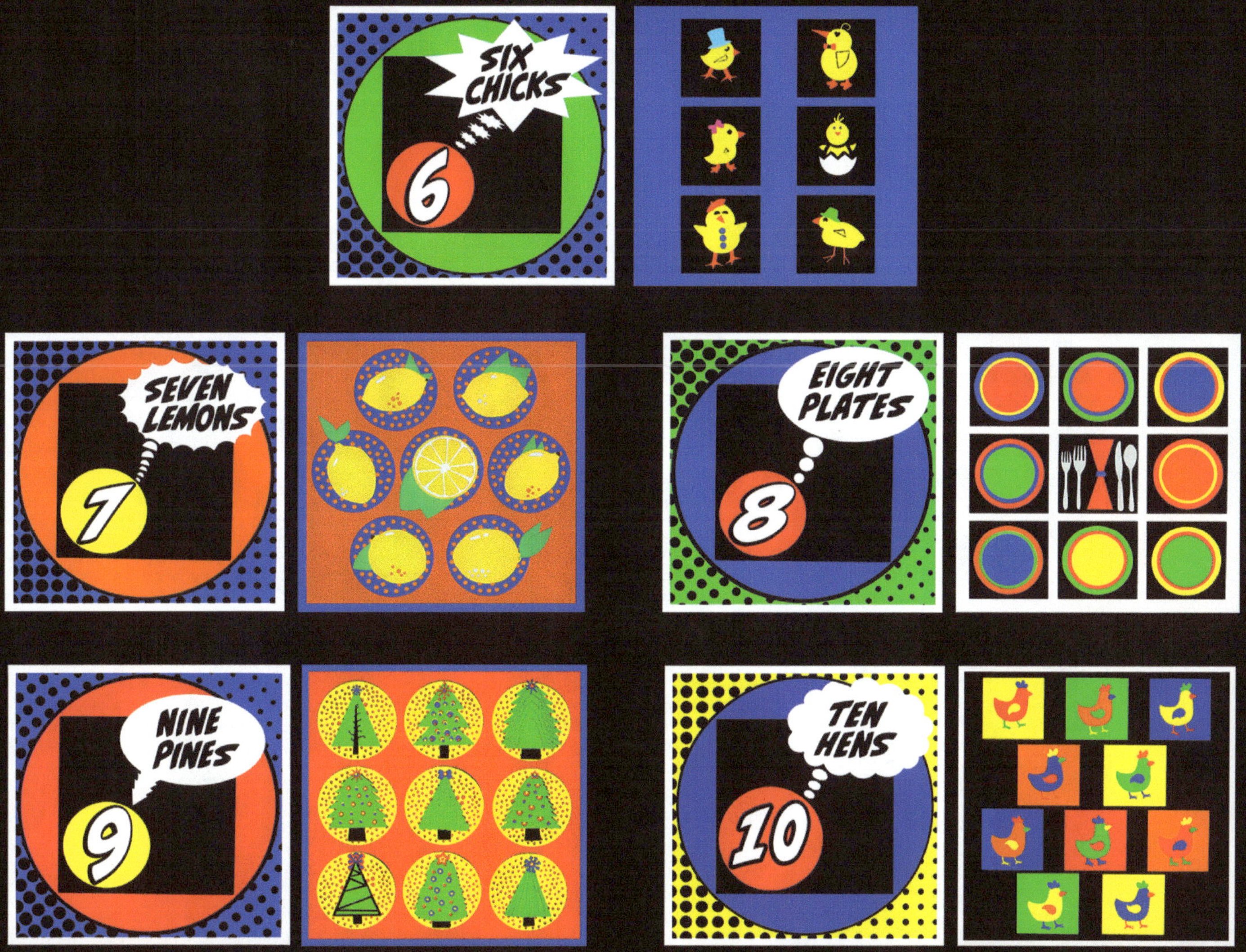
SIX CHICKS
6
SEVEN LEMONS
7
EIGHT PLATES
8
NINE PINES
9
TEN HENS
10

COME BACK SOON TO RHYME AGAIN!

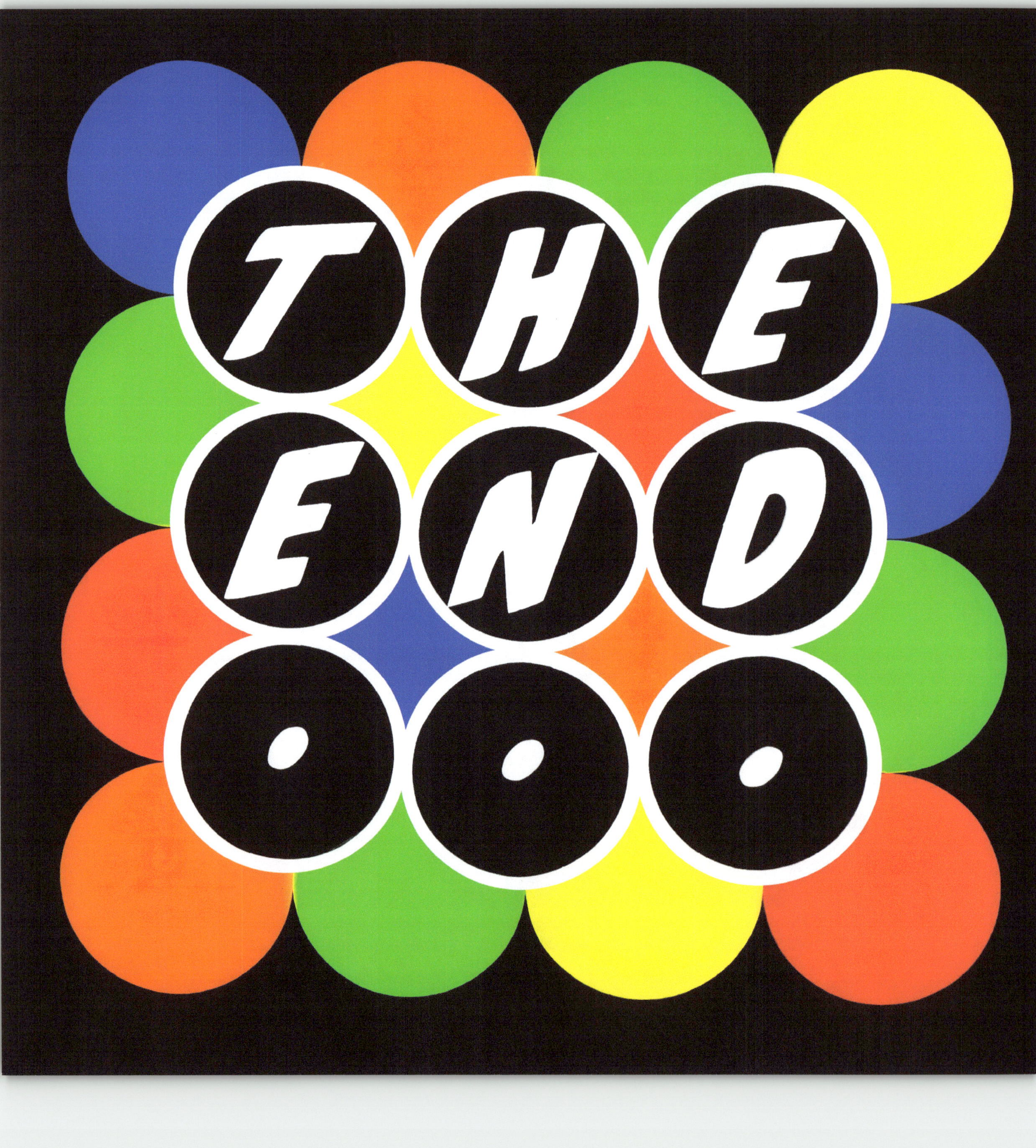
THE
END
...

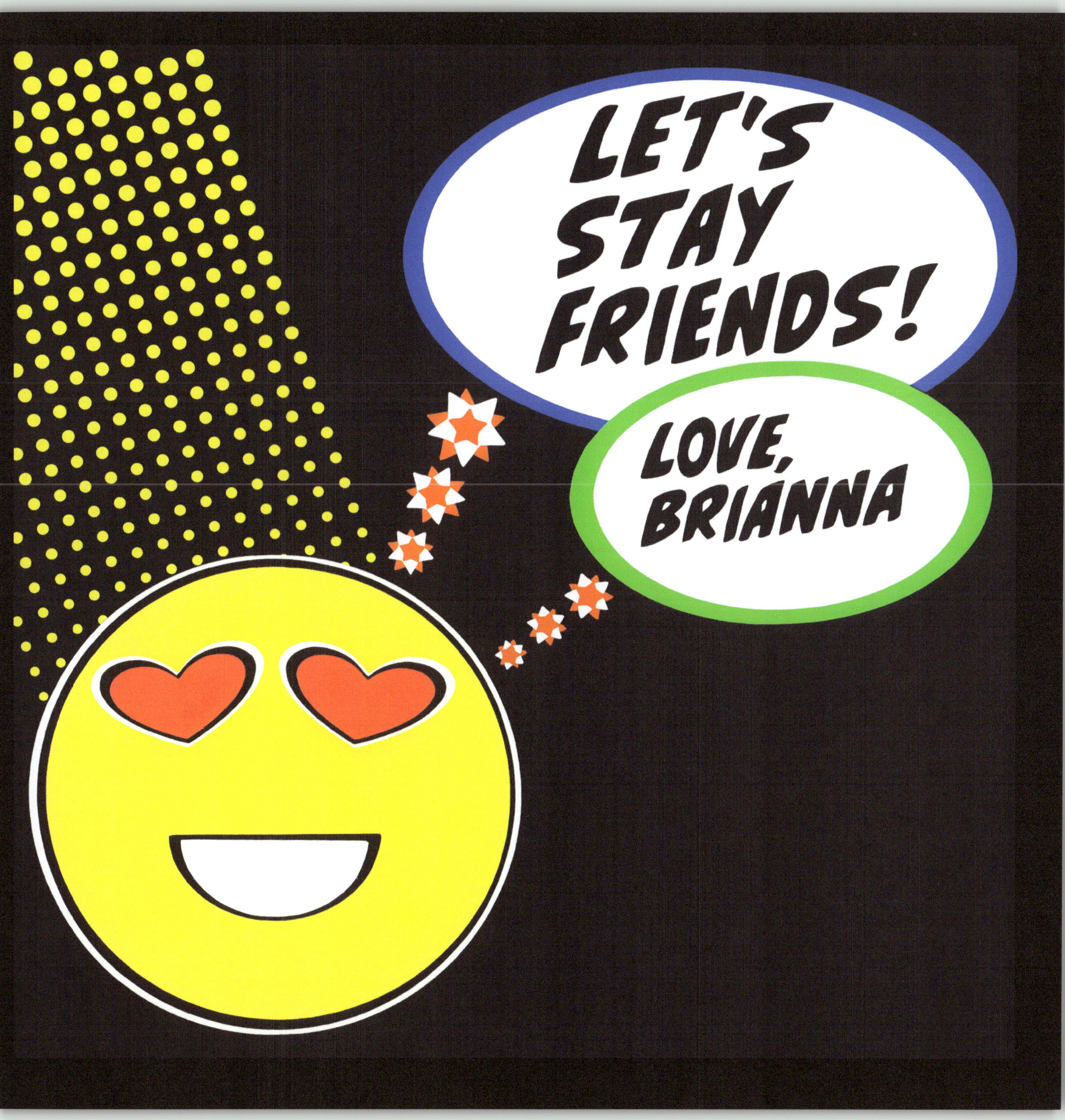
LET'S STAY FRIENDS!
LOVE, BRIANNA

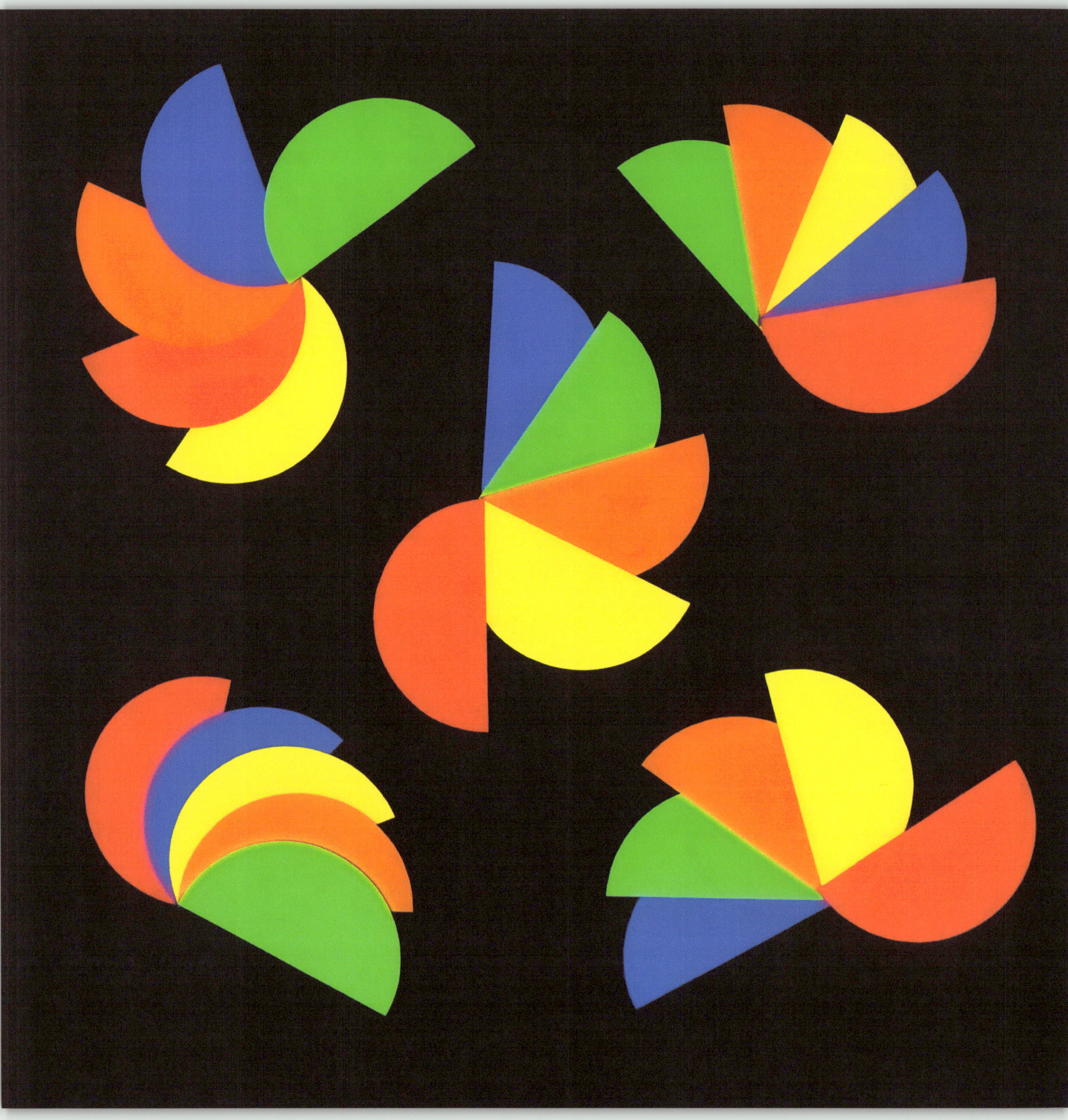

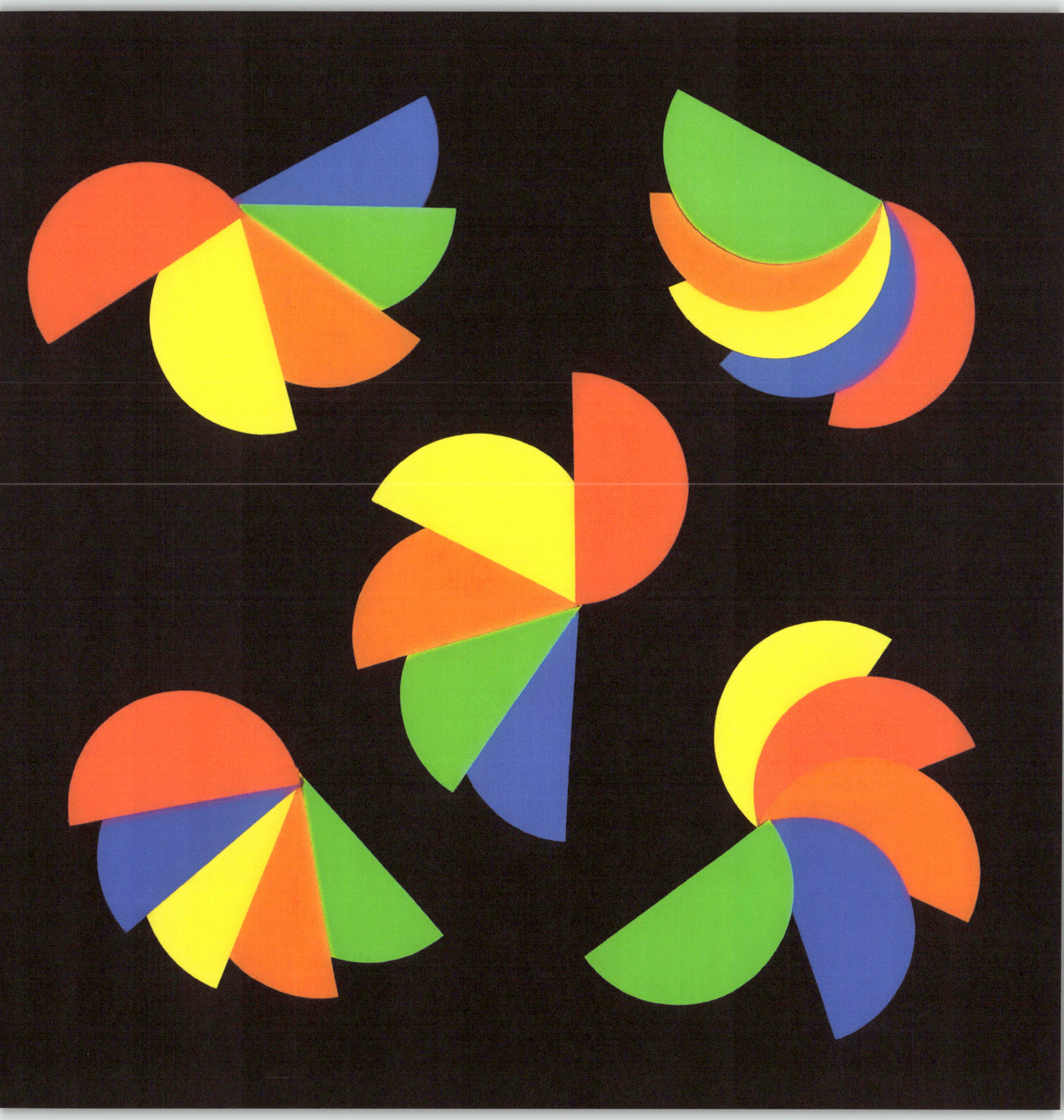

POP ART BOOKs

AVAILABLE NOW

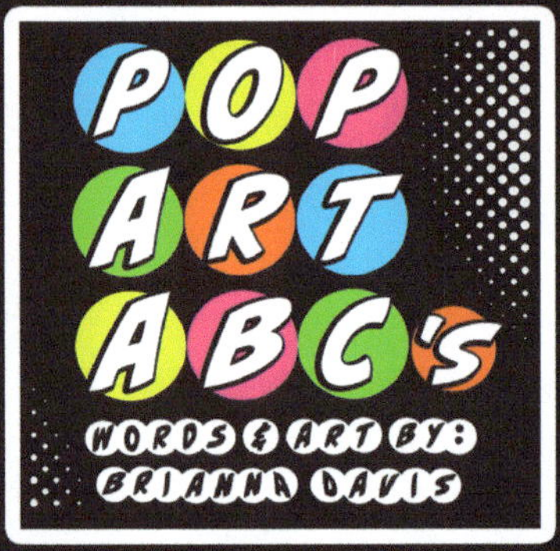
POP ART ABC's
WORDS & ART BY:
BRIANNA DAVIS

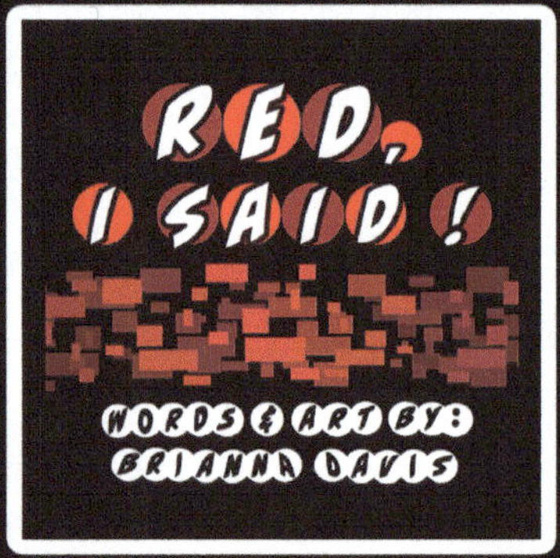
RED, I SAID!
WORDS & ART BY:
BRIANNA DAVIS

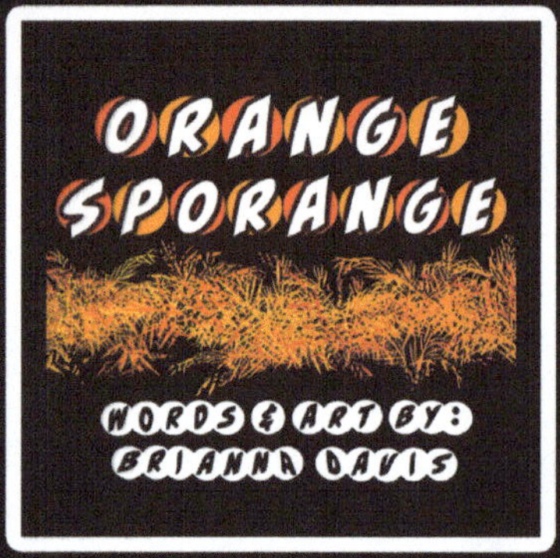
ORANGE SPORANGE
WORDS & ART BY:
BRIANNA DAVIS

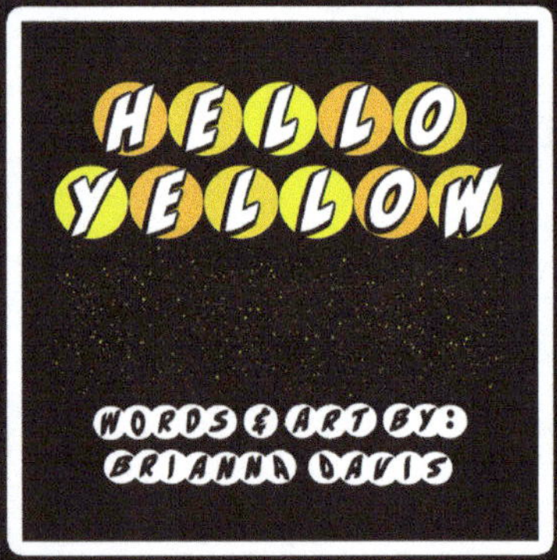
HELLO YELLOW
WORDS & ART BY:
BRIANNA DAVIS

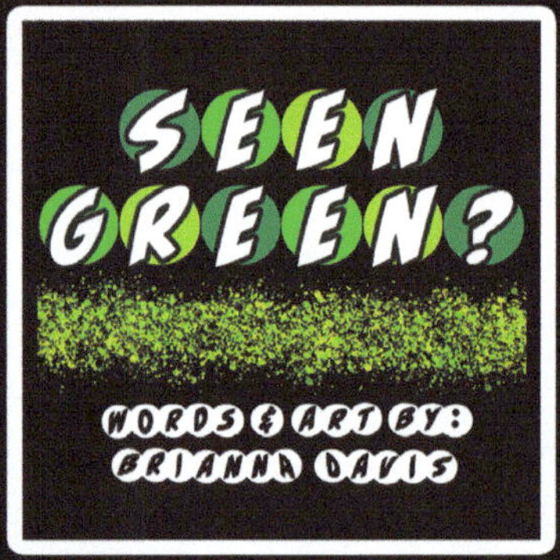
SEEN GREEN?
WORDS & ART BY:
BRIANNA DAVIS

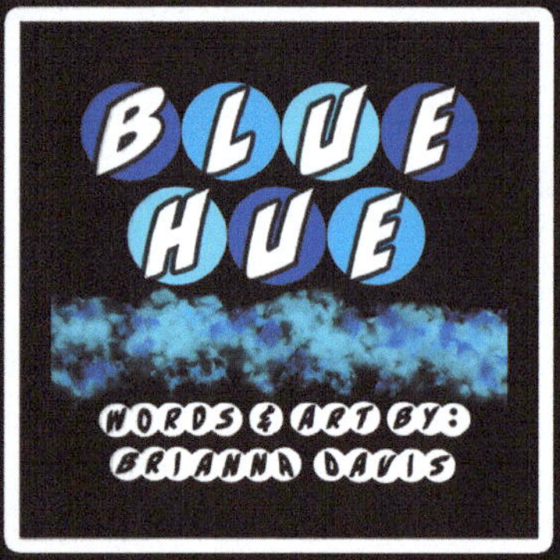
BLUE HUE
WORDS & ART BY:
BRIANNA DAVIS

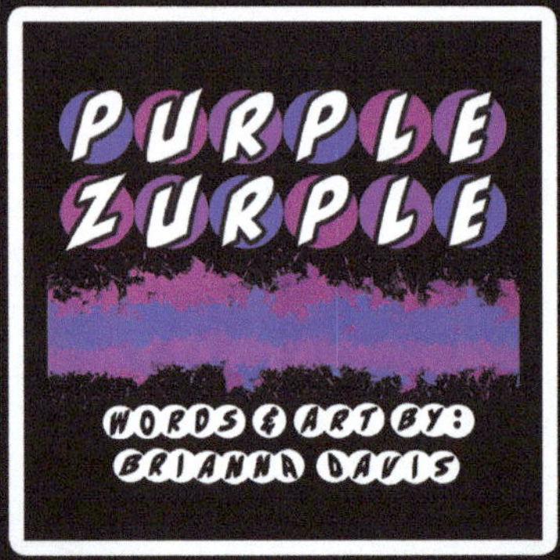
PURPLE ZURPLE
WORDS & ART BY:
BRIANNA DAVIS

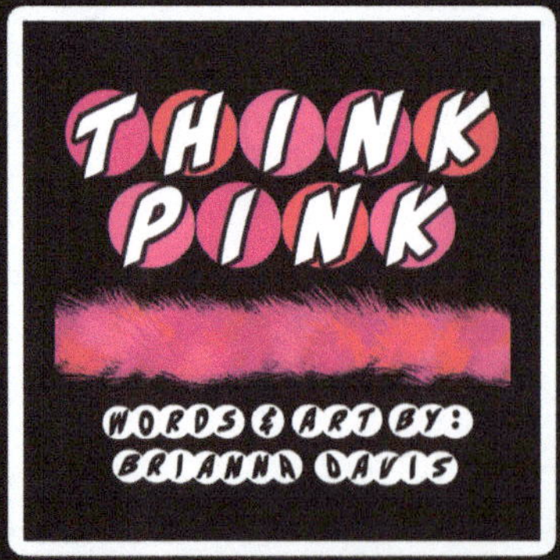
THINK PINK
WORDS & ART BY:
BRIANNA DAVIS

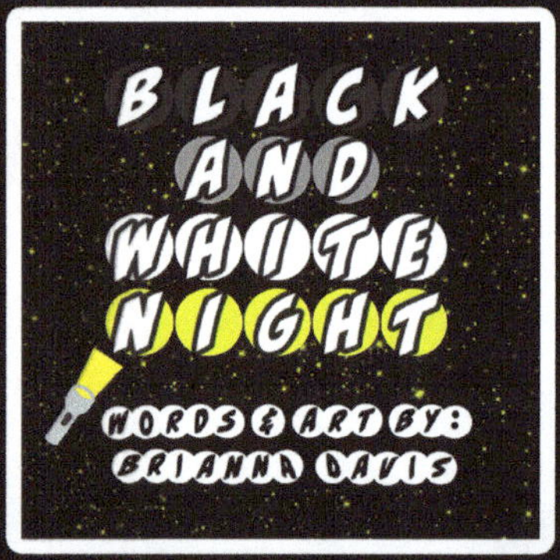
BLACK AND WHITE NIGHT
WORDS & ART BY:
BRIANNA DAVIS

www.ingramcontent.com/pod-product-compliance
Lightning Source LLC
Chambersburg PA
CBHW051825210526
45473CB00005B/1742
* 9 7 8 1 9 5 4 4 7 5 2 0 5 *